Global Cookery

Recipes from China

Dana Meachen Rau

Raintree

Raintree is an imprint of Capstone Global Library Limited, a company incorporated in England and Wales having its registered office at 7 Pilgrim Street, London, EC4V 6LB – Registered company number: 6695582

www.raintreepublishers.co.uk
myorders@raintreepublishers.co.uk

Text © Capstone Global Library Limited 2014
First published in hardback in 2014
The moral rights of the proprietor have been asserted.

Edited by Abby Colich, Laura Knowles, and John-Paul Wilkins
Designed by Cynthia Akiyoshi
Picture research by Tracy Cummins
Production by Vicki Fitzgerald
Originated by Capstone Global Library
Printed and bound in China

ISBN 978 1 406 27379 3
17 16 15 14 13
10 9 8 7 6 5 4 3 2 1

A full catalogue record for this book is available from the British Library.

Acknowledgments
We would like to thank the following for permission to reproduce photographs: Capstone Publishers pp. 1, 9–11, 16–43 (Karon Dubke); © Crown p.12 (copyright material is reproduced with the permission of HMSO and Queen's Printer for Scotland, food.gov.uk); Getty Images pp. 7 (blue jean images), 15 (Lena Granefelt); Shutterstock p. 4 (Kang Khoon Seang), 5 (TonyV3112), 6 (ValeStock), 13 (Monkey Business Images), 14 (Karlova Irina).

Design elements reproduced with permission of Shutterstock (Andrew Scherbackov, Andrey Zyk, Brooke Becker, Evlakhov Valeriy, Fedorov Oleksiy, Flavia Morlachetti, K13 ART, Luis Santos, HUANSHENG XU, marchello74, Mazzzur, Muellek Josef, Ninell, Oleg_Z, photastic, Picsfive, Richard Peterson, Sandra Cunningham, spaxiax, TungCheung).

Cover photograph of tofu with pea pods and bamboo shoots reproduced with permission of Capstone Publishers (Karon Dubke).

We would like to thank Seth Wiener, Sarah Schenker, and Marla Conn for their invaluable help in the preparation of this book.

Every effort has been made to contact copyright holders of material reproduced in this book. Any omissions will be rectified in subsequent printings if notice is given to the publishers.

Contents

Large country, long history

China is a large country covering much of southern Asia. In fact, China is the third-largest country in land area in the world. In the north, it borders Russia and Mongolia. The west and south border many countries, including India, Nepal, Myanmar (Burma), and Vietnam. The eastern edge is a coastline along the Pacific Ocean. Since China covers such a large land area, the country contains many different types of land. The Himalayas loom over China's southwest border, and contain some of the world's highest peaks. Dry deserts cover parts of the northwest. Forests grow in the south and high north. The east and south contain rich farmland.

Rice terraces, such as these in Yunnan, can be found all over China.

Not only is China's land area large. With more than a billion people, it also has the largest population in the world. Most Chinese live in villages and work as farmers. But many people also live in cities, such as Shanghai, Beijing, and Hong Kong, and work in industry.

Farmers ploughing fields with the help of oxen and workers weaving through busy city streets on bicycles are part of a culture that has existed for thousands of years. China has one of the world's oldest civilizations. Its history is divided into dynasties – periods of time ruled by emperors. This ancient country is known for its contributions to the world, such as paper, fireworks, compasses, and many other inventions. Its art and architecture, such as the written characters of calligraphy or traditional pagoda buildings, and even its food are reminders of a long past that is still an important part of China today.

Chinese city streets, such as these in Yibin, are often a hub of activity.

Nǐ chī fàn le méi? (Have you eaten?)

You can visit many Chinese restaurants outside of China. As Chinese immigrants settled in Europe and the United States, they brought their traditional foods with them. In many cities around the world, there are large Chinese communities. In China itself, food has a long history tied to its traditions, land, and people.

This street vendor in Fenghuang County, Hunan Province, is selling a tasty selection of treats!

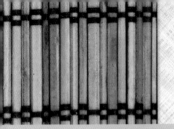

Different regions of China offer special foods. Cantonese cooking is probably the best known outside of the country. These stir-fried and steamed dishes offer lots of fresh flavours. Food from Sichuan and Hunan often contains bold spices from dried chilli peppers and Sichuan peppercorns. In the east, coastal areas have access to lots of fresh fish. Rice is eaten all over the country. Wheat is also an important grain in the north, where it is used to make steamed breads, pancakes, and dumplings. The subtropical climate of the south provides lots of fruits and vegetables.

In China, people often share dishes at mealtimes. Platters in the centre of the table hold a variety of meat and vegetable dishes. Guests serve themselves. The Chinese eat with chopsticks – two sticks that not only pick up bites of food, but can also be used to stir, mix, and serve food.

"Nǐ chī fàn le méi?" is a phrase the Chinese use to greet each other. It literally means "Have you eaten?"

Are you hungry for the fresh tastes of China?

Dumplings are a popular dish in China. Many people make them at home.

7

Chinese ingredients

Here are some ingredients found in Chinese households and in the recipes in this book. If you can't find a certain ingredient, look for similar replacements.

Rice can be cooked in many different ways and is made into rice wine, rice vinegar, and rice flour. Chinese use long-grain rice as well as glutinous rice, also known as sticky rice, for sweet dishes and treats.

Soya is another basic Chinese ingredient. Soya beans are made into blocks of soft bean curd (tofu), bean pastes, soya milk, soy sauce, and many other products.

Noodles come in many varieties. Some are made with wheat flour and others with rice flour.

Vegetables include pak choi, watercress, baby corn, aubergine, broccoli, and winter melons. Some vegetables are picked young, such as bamboo shoots, bean sprouts, and pea pods. Root vegetables include ginger, water chestnuts, ginseng, lotus, taro, radish, and turnips. Garlic and spring onions are both very common.

Chinese mushrooms include cloud ears, wood ears, black, straw, and shiitake.

Fruits include mandarin oranges, persimmons, pomelos, apples, pears, apricots, plums, dates, pineapples, lychees, and peaches.

Oils, such as peanut oil, are used to stir-fry meats and vegetables. Vegetable oil can also be used. Sesame oil adds a strong flavour. Chilli oil, flavoured with dried red chillies, adds a spicy bite.

Sauces are added to various dishes. Soy sauce comes in light and dark varieties. Plum sauce, oyster sauce, fish sauce, and hoisin sauce are also commonly used. Cornflour, mixed with water, is used to thicken sauces.

Spices include dried red chilli flakes, Sichuan peppercorns, cinnamon, and star anise. Chinese five-spice powder is a blend of cinnamon, cloves, Sichuan peppercorns, fennel, and star anise.

Fresh herbs include coriander leaves (also known as cilantro), lemongrass, and chives.

Nuts include peanuts, cashews, almonds, walnuts, chestnuts, and ginkgo nuts.

Meat in China often means pork. Beef is popular in the west, and lamb in the north. Chicken and duck are the common poultry.

Fish is caught fresh in both rivers and ocean. These include carp, eels, and shellfish such as crabs, prawns, lobster, and scallops.

Wrappers, or thin sheets of dough, are sold to make wontons and other types of dumplings. Wontons and dumplings are pockets filled with meat or vegetables that can be steamed, fried, or boiled.

Drying and pickling are methods used to preserve some foods. These foods include dried red chillies, mushrooms, tangerine peel, seaweed, Sichuan pickles, and winter pickles.

Sweetness is added to dishes with white sugar, brown sugar, rock sugar (like sticks of rock), and honey. Sweetened red bean paste is used in buns and dumplings.

The Chinese diet is filled with a variety of healthy foods.

How to use this book

Each chapter of this book will introduce you to aspects of Chinese cooking. But you don't have to read the book from beginning to end. Flip through, find what interests you, and give it a try. You may discover a recipe that becomes your new favourite meal!

If you already do a lot of cooking, you may know your way around the kitchen. But if you've never stir-fried ginger, folded a wonton, or flipped a pancake, don't worry. Have a look at the glossary on page 44.

Zǎoshàng hǎo (Good morning)

Before heading out to school or work for the day, Chinese families might eat rice porridge, one of the most popular morning meals. Others might eat an egg or a pancake with a glass of soya milk. These morning treats are also enjoyed as side dishes or snacks at other times of the day.

Congee

Congee is a porridge made of rice. The rice cooks for a long time so the grains break up into a soft, thick soup. Congee is a comfort food in China. People may eat it to help them feel better when they are ill.

Ingredients	Tools
100 g jasmine rice	Stockpot
950 ml water	Mixing spoon

16

Each recipe is set up the same way: Ingredients lists all the ingredients you'll need for the recipe. Tools tells you the various kitchen utensils you will need. Collect the ingredients and tools before you start working so that you have everything nearby when you need it.

Then just follow the Steps. Make sure you read them carefully. Numbers on the photos indicate which step they refer to. Don't worry if your creation isn't perfect when you reach the end. Cooking takes practice and experimentation. Be patient and enjoy the process.

If you have to follow a specific diet, or have food allergies, look for the labels on each recipe. These will tell you if a dish is vegan, vegetarian, dairy-free, gluten-free, or if it contains nuts. However, you should always check food packaging before use to be sure.

Steps

1. Combine the rice and water in a stockpot. Bring to the boil. Then reduce the heat to low.

2. Cook covered for about 60 to 90 minutes, until the rice breaks down and softens. Stir frequently to prevent the rice from sticking to the bottom of the pot. Serve warm.

Quick tip

Eating with chopsticks can be tricky. But the more you practise, the easier it will get.

- Hold the top chopstick with the tips of your thumb and index finger.
- Hold the bottom stick between the tips of your middle and ring finger.
- Open and close the chopsticks with your index finger.

VARIATION

Congee can be eaten plain, but usually condiments are added. You can cook the rice in vegetable or chicken stock instead of water. Top it with pieces of cooked chicken or fish, or bite-size vegetables. Sichuan pickled vegetables are one of the most popular toppings (see recipe on page 26).

N contains **uts**

D airy free

G luten free

V egetarian

V egan

D airy free   **V** egetarian   **V** egan   **G** luten free

Makes 2 servings
Time: 60 to 90 minutes

17

Look at Quick tips for cooking and kitchen advice, and Variations for swapping ingredients for others if you would like.

Whenever you are in the kitchen, ask an adult to help or be nearby. You shouldn't use any knife or appliance without an adult's permission and assistance. You can find more ways to be safe while you cook on page 14.

A healthy kitchen

It's fun to head out on a food adventure by trying new tastes from countries beyond your own. But you should also keep your health in mind. The following are the basic food groups. The Chinese include these groups in a meal, or over the course of a day, to get the proper balance of nutrients to grow and be healthy.

Fruits and vegetables

Fruit in China, from mandarin oranges to Asian pears, are enjoyed as a sweet flavour in a balanced meal. Vegetables are also a very important part of the Chinese diet. They are cooked in stir-fries and used as dumpling fillings. Both fruits and vegetables can help reduce the risk of getting certain diseases. They contain nutrients your body needs and fibre to keep your digestive system running smoothly.

The eatwell plate

FOOD STANDARDS AGENCY
food.gov.uk

Use the eatwell plate to help you get the balance right. It shows how much of what you eat should come from each food group.

Fruit and vegetables

Bread, rice, potatoes, pasta and other starchy foods

Meat, fish, eggs, beans and other non-dairy sources of protein

Foods and drinks high in fat and/or sugar

Milk and dairy foods

The eatwell plate shows us the importance of eating a combination of all the food groups in our diets.

Try eating your Chinese meals with chopsticks! See how to use them on page 17.

Grains

These are foods made from wheat, rice, corn, or other grains. Whole grains that use the entire grain kernel are the healthiest. Refined grains, such as white flour and white rice, do not have as many vitamins and minerals. Rice is the main grain of China. Wheat is also a part of Chinese cuisine.

Protein

Protein foods include meat, poultry, seafood, and eggs. The Chinese also get protein from soya and nuts.

Dairy

Milk and any products made from milk fall into this category. Dairy foods contain a lot of bone-building calcium. The Chinese, however, do not normally eat dairy products. But they do get calcium from many sources, such as leafy green vegetables, oranges, almonds, sesame seeds, and soya beans.

Fats and sugar

Some oils, especially the ones from plants like peanut, vegetable, and sesame oil, do provide some important nutrients. Nuts are high in oils, too. But solid fats, such as meat fat, are not as good for you. So use them sparingly. Your body needs sugar, but not too much. Try not to fill up on too many Chinese treats with added sugar.

A safe kitchen

It's fun to whip up a tasty new creation in the kitchen, but safety should be your number one concern. Here are some tips to keep in mind:

- Make sure an adult is nearby for permission, help, advice, and assistance.

- Wash your hands before you work.

- Wear the right clothing, including sturdy shoes and an apron.

- Foods can grow harmful bacteria. Make sure you keep foods in the refrigerator or freezer until they are ready to use. Check expiration dates. If something smells or looks funny, it may be spoiled.

Make sure you cut carefully and always use a chopping board.

- Raw meat, poultry, seafood, and eggs can carry germs. Always wash your hands immediately after touching them. Wash any knife or chopping board after you use them. Make sure these foods are cooked all the way through before you eat them. Clean worktops and kitchen tools with warm, soapy water when you have finished working.

- On the hob, make sure pan handles don't stick out, so the pans don't get knocked over. Never leave pans unattended. Do not let anything flammable, such as loose sleeves or tea towels, near burners on the hob.

Remember to rinse fruits and vegetables before you use them.

- Always use oven gloves when removing something from the oven or microwave. Avoid steam when you lift a top off a pan on the hob or in the oven.

- Knives are sharp. Always point the blade away from you. Take your time and pay attention to what you are cutting. Don't use a knife without the help of an adult.

Zǎoshàng hǎo (Good morning)

Before heading out to school or work for the day, Chinese families might eat rice porridge, one of the most popular morning meals. Others might eat an egg or a pancake with a glass of soya milk. These morning treats are also enjoyed as side dishes or snacks at other times of the day.

Congee

Congee is a porridge made of rice. The rice cooks for a long time so the grains break up into a soft, thick soup. Congee is a comfort food in China. People may eat it to help them feel better when they are ill.

Ingredients

100 g jasmine rice
950 ml water

Tools

Stockpot
Mixing spoon

Steps

1. Combine the rice and water in a stockpot. Bring to the boil. Then reduce the heat to low.

2. Cook covered for about 60 to 90 minutes, until the rice breaks down and softens. Stir frequently to prevent the rice from sticking to the bottom of the pot. Serve warm.

Quick tip

Eating with chopsticks can be tricky. But the more you practise, the easier it will get.

- Hold the top chopstick with the tips of your thumb and index finger.

- Hold the bottom stick between the tips of your middle and ring finger.

- Open and close the chopsticks with your index finger.

VARIATION

Congee can be eaten plain, but usually condiments are added. You can cook the rice in vegetable or chicken stock instead of water. Top it with pieces of cooked chicken or fish, or bite-size vegetables. Sichuan pickled vegetables are one of the most popular toppings (see recipe on page 26).

Dairy free **V**egetarian **V**egan **G**luten free

Makes 2 servings
Time: 60 to 90 minutes

Spring onion pancakes

Each bite of these round, savoury treats is packed with spring onions. Spring onions are often used in Chinese cooking. The green ends used in this dish should be sliced thin to create little rings. You can serve these pancakes with soy sauce for dipping.

Ingredients

300 g flour

1 teaspoon salt

240 ml boiling water

4 to 5 spring onions, thinly
  sliced, green parts only

1 tablespoon sesame oil
  (for brushing)

1 tablespoon peanut oil
  (for frying)

Tools

Kitchen scales

Bowl

Mixing spoon

Measuring jug
  and spoons

Damp towel

Rolling pin

Pastry brush

Frying pan

Spatula

Knife

Chopping board

Baking tray

Steps

1. Mix the flour and salt in a large bowl. Add half of the boiling water, stirring well. Add the rest of the water a little at a time. Let it cool slightly, and then use your hands to shape the dough into a ball.

2. Turn the dough out onto a floured surface and knead it for about a minute until smooth. Cover it with a damp towel and let it rest for about 30 minutes.

3. Sprinkle flour on your work surface and knead the dough about 10 times. Then cut it into 4 equal pieces.

4. With the rolling pin, roll one piece of the dough out into a thin disc. Brush it with sesame oil. Sprinkle with spring onion.

5. Starting at one end of the disc, roll the dough up into a tube shape. Then coil the tube into a circle.

6. Flatten the coil with your hand and roll it out with the rolling pin again into a thin, flat disc, about 15 to 18 centimetres across.

7. Heat the peanut oil in a frying pan on medium high. Fry the pancake on one side for 1 to 2 minutes. Flip over with a spatula, and cook on the other side for 1 or 2 minutes. Set on a baking tray in an oven set at 100°C to keep warm while you cook the rest of the pancakes.

8. Cut into wedges to serve.

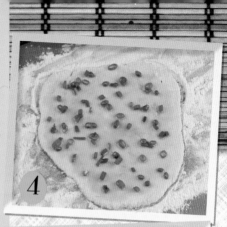

4

5

Makes 4 servings
Time: About 1 hour

contains
Nuts

Vegan

Dairy
free

Vegetarian

19

Tea eggs

The Chinese have been drinking tea for thousands of years. The flavour of tea is also a nice addition to eggs. Your kitchen will fill with the aromas of China while the eggs steep in a fragrant mixture. Tea eggs are sold at shops throughout the country.

Ingredients

6 large eggs
Water for boiling
1 litre water for steeping
Leaves from 2 black tea bags
5 tablespoons soy sauce
1 tablespoon white sugar
1 cinnamon stick
2 star anise

Tools

Stockpot
Spoon or fork
Measuring jug and spoons

Steps

1. Place the eggs in a stockpot and fill with water so all the eggs are covered. Bring to the boil. Reduce the heat, cover, and simmer for about 12 minutes.

2. Pour the hot water out of the pot, and fill again with cold water. Repeat until the eggs are cool enough to handle.

3. Lightly tap the eggs all over with the back of a spoon or fork. This will make small cracks all around the eggs, but the shells will still be attached to the eggs.

4. Refill the stockpot with 1 litre of fresh water. Add the soy sauce, tea, sugar, cinnamon, and star anise. Place the eggs into this mixture.

5. Heat to boiling over high heat, then reduce the heat and simmer uncovered for about 2 hours.

6. Drain the eggs, rinse to cool, and unpeel the shells to reveal the cracked patterns beneath.

 Gluten free **V**egetarian **D**airy free

Makes 3 servings (2 eggs each)
Time: About 2½ hours

Small bites

The Chinese often sit down to three meals a day. But they also enjoy small bites in between. Street vendors sell snacks of meat, bowls of soup, or a plate of dumplings. Before a meal, a host might place some small snacks on the table, such as peanuts. During a meal, condiments, such as pickled vegetables, can be added to a dish.

Five-spice peanuts

There are five basic tastes in Chinese food: salty, sweet, sour, spicy, and bitter. This recipe combines this variety of flavours into one snack by using Chinese five-spice powder. A popular snack in China, peanuts are often boiled or fried. Here, they are baked.

Ingredients	Tools
2 tablespoons five-spice powder	Resealable plastic bag
½ teaspoon salt	Kitchen scales
1 egg white, beaten	Measuring spoons
1 teaspoon orange zest	Bowl
300 g unsalted roasted peanuts	Mixing spoon
Non-stick cooking spray	Whisk
	Baking tray

Steps

1. Preheat oven to 170°C.

2. In a resealable plastic bag, combine the five-spice powder, salt, and orange zest.

3. In a bowl, beat the egg white with a whisk. Add the nuts and stir well until the nuts are moist.

4. Pour the nuts into the bag of spices. Seal the bag, and shake it to evenly coat the nuts with spices.

5. Spray a baking tray with non-stick cooking spray. Pour the nuts onto the baking tray so they form a single layer.

6. Bake for about 20 to 25 minutes. Halfway through baking, swish the nuts around with a spoon to make sure they aren't sticking.

7. Allow to cool before serving.

Makes 6-8 servings as a snack
Time: About 30 minutes

Quick tip

Orange zest is the skin of an orange. To zest an orange for this recipe, rub a grater with small holes across the skin to grate it into tiny strips.

Nuts contains   **G**luten free   **D**airy free

Vegetarian

VARIATIONS

You can make this snack with other popular Chinese nuts, such as cashews or walnuts.

Barbecue spare ribs

This Cantonese dish is prepared by roasting pork ribs that are slathered in a sweet, smoky sauce. Here, we use a slow cooker to help the ribs absorb the flavours and make the meat tender. Broiling them briefly before and after helps add a crisp layer.

Ingredients	Sauce	Tools
1.4 kg spare ribs	8 tablespoons hoisin sauce	Knife
Non-stick cooking spray	3 tablespoons soy sauce	Chopping board
	3 tablespoons honey	Grill pan
	3 tablespoons rice vinegar	Bowl
	2 teaspoons sesame oil	Whisk
	3 garlic cloves, chopped	Baking dish
	½ teaspoon salt	Tongs
	½ teaspoon pepper	Baster
	240 ml chicken stock	Kitchen foil

Makes 6 to 8 servings as an appetizer
Time: 15 minutes prep, 3 hours to cook

Gluten free   **D**airy free

Steps

1. If not already divided, cut the meat into individual ribs.

2. Spray the grill pan with non-stick spray. Place the ribs on the pan, and grill for about 15 minutes, flipping once during cooking, to brown the outside.

3. Meanwhile, in a bowl, whisk together the sauce ingredients.

4. Place the ribs in a baking dish. Pour about half of the sauce over the ribs. Set the oven to 180°C. Place the ribs on the centre rack of the oven.

5. Cook the ribs for 3 hours, uncovered for the first 1½ hours and covered with foil the second 1½ hours. Every 30 minutes during cooking, flip the ribs over with tongs, and baste them with sauce. Add a little more sauce each time to keep the ribs from drying out.

6. If you want to make these ribs into a meal, serve with rice (see Quick tip on page 33) and cucumber sticks.

Sichuan pickled vegetables

The people of Sichuan pickle vegetables by preserving them in vinegar and spices. Pickled vegetables add a spicy kick to mild dishes, such as congee, or a burst of flavour to other meals. If you can't find Sichuan peppercorns, you can use black peppercorns. The flavour is different, but they will still add heat to your pickles!

Ingredients

1 cucumber	2 slices fresh root ginger
5 radishes	2 teaspoons salt
100 g shredded cabbage	1 teaspoon sugar
120 ml rice vinegar	½ teaspoon red chilli flakes
120 ml water, plus more for filling	1 teaspoon Sichuan peppercorns

Tools

Knife
Chopping board
Kitchen scales
Measuring jug
Bowl
Mixing spoon
1 empty (1-litre) jar with lid (or a few smaller-sized jars)
Saucepan
Vegetable peeler

Steps

1. Peel and seed the cucumber. Cut into 2.5-centimetre strips. Slice the radishes into small pieces. Combine in a bowl. Add the shredded cabbage. Stir to combine.

2. Fill the jar (or jars) to the top with the vegetable mixture.

3. In a small saucepan, heat the water, vinegar, ginger slices, salt, sugar, red chilli flakes, and peppercorns. Bring to the boil. Stir for a few minutes until the sugar and salt are dissolved.

4. Pour the heated mixture into the jar (or divide the mixture among the jars) over the vegetables. Keep the ginger slices in the jar, too, to add flavour.

5. Add cold water until all of the vegetables are covered with liquid. Stir it with a spoon.

6. Let the jar cool, uncovered, to room temperature. Then twist on the lid and refrigerate the pickles for at least 24 hours before eating. They will get spicier the longer they sit. Serve with congee (see recipe on page 16), or alongside any Chinese dish as a condiment.

Gluten free **D**airy free **V**egetarian **V**egan

Makes 1 (1-litre) jar of vegetables

Time: About 20 minutes, at least 24 hours in the refrigerator. Eat within a week.

27

Vegetable wonton soup

Wontons are dumplings filled with pork, prawns, or vegetables. Wontons can be boiled, steamed, or deep-fried. To eat them in a soup, bring the bowl close to your mouth, and use your chopsticks to hold the wonton to take a bite. You can sip the soup right from the bowl.

Ingredients

Wontons

- 1 packet wonton wrappers
- 200 g shredded cabbage
- 100 g shredded carrots
- 100 g sliced mushrooms
- 4 to 5 spring onions, thinly sliced, white parts
- 30 g minced water chestnuts
- 2 teaspoons minced root ginger
- ½ teaspoon rice wine vinegar
- ½ teaspoon sesame oil
- ¼ teaspoon sugar
- ¼ teaspoon salt

Soup

- 900 ml chicken stock
- 2 slices fresh root ginger
- 4 to 5 spring onions, thinly sliced, green parts
- ½ teaspoon sesame oil

Tools

- Kitchen scales
- Measuring jug
- Stockpot
- Slotted spoon
- Colander
- Kitchen roll
- Knife
- Chopping board
- Bowl
- Cling film
- Spoon
- Baking tray
- Ladle
- Four serving bowls
- Greaseproof paper

Steps

1. In a stockpot, bring about 2 litres of water to the boil. Add the cabbage, carrots, and sliced mushrooms. Return to the boil, then remove the vegetables with a slotted spoon into a bowl. Immediately rinse with cold water.

2. Wrap the drained vegetables in kitchen roll and squeeze to remove all the liquid. Place the vegetables on a chopping board and chop very finely.

3. Combine the chopped vegetables, spring onions, water chestnuts, and ginger in a bowl. Add the vinegar, sesame oil, sugar, and salt, and mix well. Cover with cling film and refrigerate for about 30 minutes.

4. To fill the wontons, spoon a little of the filling into the centre of a wonton wrapper. Dip your finger in water and run along the edges to wet the wrapper. Fold the wrapper in half and squeeze all around the edges to seal.

5. Wet one of the corners and tuck it under the opposite one. Squeeze to seal. Place the wontons on a baking tray lined with greaseproof paper and cover with damp kitchen roll to stop them from drying out.

6. Fill a stockpot halfway with water and bring to the boil. Add the wontons. When they float to the top, they are cooked. It will take about 3 minutes. Place a few in each serving bowl.

7. For the soup, bring the chicken stock and the sliced ginger to the boil in the stockpot. Lower heat and simmer for about 5 minutes.

8. Add the sesame oil. Ladle the stock over the wontons. Sprinkle with spring onion greens to finish.

Makes about 30 wontons
(4 to 6 servings)
Time: About 2 hours total

Dairy free

29

The ancient wok

The wok is the basic piece of cooking equipment that has been used in China for thousands of years. Chinese people use the wok for one of the most popular and quickest methods of cooking – stir-frying. To stir-fry, you cook ginger, garlic, vegetables, and meat in a little oil, constantly stirring and tossing them while they cook. You can add sauces and spices as you go. Stir-frying helps keep the vegetables colourful, crispy, fresh, and nutritious.

If you don't have a wok, you can use a frying pan instead. Be careful, though. Oil can splatter and burn if you don't pay close attention while you are cooking.

Kung Pao chicken

The origin of Kung Pao chicken is uncertain. One legend says that it was the favourite dish of a Sichuan governor in the late 1800s. It is said that after trying the dish, he liked it so much that he had it named after him! Whatever the case, this is a delicious dish, and remains one of the most popular Chinese dishes outside of China.

Ingredients

450 g boneless chicken breasts, cut into 1.5-cm cubes

2 teaspoons cornflour mixed with 1 tablespoon water

1 teaspoon rice wine vinegar

1 tablespoon peanut oil

5 to 6 spring onions, thinly sliced, white parts only

4 garlic cloves, minced

2 teaspoons minced root ginger

About 8 to 10 dried red chillies, seeded (or ½ teaspoon red chilli flakes)

50 g unsalted dry roasted peanuts

Sauce

2 teaspoons soy sauce

2 teaspoons Chinese black vinegar (or balsamic vinegar)

1 teaspoon sesame oil

2 teaspoons sugar

1 teaspoon ground Sichuan pepper

Tools

Kitchen scales

Measuring spoons

Bowl

Whisk

Frying pan

Mixing spoon

Steps

1. In a bowl, whisk together the cornflour, water, and rice vinegar. Add the chicken pieces and mix until well coated. Set aside to marinate for about 15 minutes.

2. In another bowl, whisk together the sauce ingredients.

3. Heat the peanut oil in the frying pan. Add the marinated chicken and stir-fry for about 3 to 4 minutes until it cooks through.

4. Add the spring onions, garlic, ginger, and red chillies. Stir-fry for 45 seconds.

Quick tip

Cutting meat into small, bite-size pieces makes it cook quickly, and also makes it easier to pick up with chopsticks. Kitchen scissors can be used to cut the meat.

5. Add the sauce and stir well so the chicken is coated. Sprinkle in the peanuts and stir to combine. Serve with rice (see Quick tip on page 33).

Ncontains **N**uts   **D**airy free   **G**luten free   Makes 4 servings
Time: About 30 minutes

31

Sweet and sour pork

The Chinese have an ancient belief that yin and yang (forces in the universe) must be in balance. Mixing various flavours and textures in a dish or a meal makes it a balanced meal. This could be a mix of cool and warm flavours, or soft and crunchy textures. The opposite tastes of sweet and sour are in balance in this classic dish.

Ingredients

350 g pork tenderloin, cut into 1.5-cm strips

75 g flour

Salt and pepper, to taste

2 tablespoons peanut oil, divided

6 to 7 spring onions, thinly sliced, white parts only

1 red pepper, seeded and cut into squares

2 garlic cloves, minced

1 teaspoon minced root ginger

1 teaspoon cornflour mixed with ½ tablespoon water

1 (400-g) can pineapple chunks in juice

Sauce

2 tablespoons soy sauce

3 tablespoons white distilled vinegar

3 tablespoons brown sugar

1 teaspoon sesame oil

2 tablespoons tomato paste

120 ml pineapple juice (from the canned pineapple chunks)

Tools

Kitchen scales
Measuring jug
Bowls
Whisk
Frying pan
Mixing spoon

Steps

1. In a bowl, toss together the flour and salt and pepper. Add the pork pieces and toss with the flour until well coated. Set aside.

2. Whisk together the sauce ingredients. Set aside.

3. In the frying pan, heat 1 tablespoon peanut oil. Add the pork and stir-fry for about 3 to 4 minutes until mostly cooked through. Remove the pork from the pan and set aside.

4. Heat another tablespoon of peanut oil in the pan. Add the spring onions and red pepper. Stir-fry for 2 minutes. Add the ginger and garlic and stir-fry for about 1 more minute.

5. Add the pineapple chunks and the sauce. Bring to the boil. Add the pork back in, and let it all cook together for another 2 minutes.

6. Stir in the cornflour and water mixture. Cook for another minute or until the pork is cooked through and the sauce has thickened. Serve with rice (see Quick tip, right).

Quick tip

Rice is the perfect addition to a stir-fry dish. Rice helps balance an especially spicy dish. It also absorbs the sauce.

To make rice, follow the directions on the packet. You may need to rinse the rice first, to wash off the extra starch. Keep the lid on the saucepan while the rice absorbs the water. Before serving, fluff it with chopsticks to separate the grains.

Ncontains **uts**   **D**airy free

Makes 4 servings
Time: About 20 minutes

Tofu with pea pods and bamboo shoots

Some Chinese dishes use bean curd (tofu) as the main protein instead of meat. Tofu does not have a lot of flavour on its own. It absorbs the flavours it is cooked with. This stir-fry dish also uses tasty vegetables – the young, tender shoots of bamboo and crispy, green pea pods.

Ingredients

- 1 (400-g) packet medium-firm tofu, drained
- 5 to 6 spring onions, thinly sliced, white and green parts separated
- 2 teaspoons minced root ginger
- 1 (225-g) can bamboo shoots, rinsed and drained
- 100 g pea pods
- 1 tablespoon peanut oil
- 2 teaspoons cornflour mixed with 1 tablespoon water

Sauce

- 1 tablespoon soy sauce
- 120 ml vegetable stock
- 1 teaspoon brown sugar

Tools

- Knife
- Chopping board
- Kitchen scales
- Measuring jug
- Whisk
- Frying pan
- Mixing spoon or spatula

Steps

1. Cut the tofu into 1.5-centimetre cubes. Prepare the spring onions, ginger, bamboo shoots, and pea pods. Whisk together the sauce ingredients. Set aside.

2. Heat the peanut oil in the frying pan. Add the ginger and white parts of the spring onions. Stir-fry for about 1 minute.

3. Add the cubes of tofu. Stir-fry them for another 2 minutes, stirring gently.

4. Add the bamboo shoots and pea pods. Stir-fry for another minute.

5. Add the sauce and stir to coat. Pour in the cornflour and water mixture. Cook for another minute, gently stirring until the sauce thickens slightly.

6. Sprinkle with the green parts of the spring onions. Serve with rice (see Quick tip on page 33).

Quick tip

Stir-frying is a quick process. That's why it's important to prepare all of your ingredients ahead of time. Before you heat the oil, cut your vegetables and meat or tofu, and mix your sauces. Then they are ready to add when you need them.

VARIATION

If you are not a fan of bamboo shoots or pea pods, you can add any vegetable you want to this dish. Try broccoli, baby corn, or pak choi. Toss in water chestnuts to add a fresh crunch.

Vegetarian **N**uts contains

Vegan **D**airy free **G**luten free

Makes 4 to 6 servings with rice
Time: About 15 minutes

Fàn and miàn (Rice and noodles)

Rice (called *fàn*) is a handy ingredient in Chinese cuisine. It can be served for breakfast, lunch, dinner, and snacks. It can be steamed, boiled, and fried. Noodles (*miàn*) are also an easy base for vegetables, meat, and flavourings.

Fried rice

Fried rice is a Cantonese dish. It's a quick and easy way to make a meal using leftovers. Peas are used here, but you can add any type of small, diced vegetable.

Ingredients

1 teaspoon & 1 tablespoon vegetable oil, divided

2 eggs, beaten

3 thin slices fresh root ginger

50 g frozen green peas, thawed

50 g finely diced cooked ham

½ teaspoon sugar

2 tablespoons soy sauce

3 cups cooked rice

2 spring onions, thinly sliced

Black pepper, to taste

Tools

Frying pan

Mixing spoon

Whisk

Steps

1. Heat 1 teaspoon of oil in the frying pan. Add the beaten eggs. Scramble them for about 1 minute, breaking them into small bits as you cook. Remove from the pan and set aside.

2. Heat 1 tablespoon of oil in the pan. Add the ginger and peas. Stir-fry for about 1 minute.

3. Add the ham, sugar, and soy sauce. Stir-fry for about 2 minutes.

4. Stir in the rice and fry for about 2 more minutes.

5. Take the pan off the heat. Add the cooked eggs and spring onions. Add pepper to taste.

Quick tip

To beat an egg, break the egg into a bowl. With a fork or a whisk, stir quickly in a circular motion until the yolk and white are fully blended together.

Dairy free   **G**luten free

Makes 4 servings
Time: About 30 minutes

Dan dan noodles

Dan dan noodles are a traditional street food in Sichuan. They get their name from the bamboo poles, called *dan*, that vendors wear over their shoulders. Hanging from these poles are baskets holding the pots, stoves, and sauces used to make the noodles.

Ingredients

1 (300-g) packet Chinese noodles
1 tablespoon peanut oil
1 teaspoon minced root ginger
2 garlic cloves, minced
225 g ground pork
Salt

Sauce

2 tablespoons soy sauce
1 teaspoon sesame oil
2 teaspoons rice vinegar
¼ teaspoon red chilli flakes (or more if you like it spicy!)
½ teaspoon Sichuan pepper
½ teaspoon sugar
3 to 4 spring onions, thinly sliced, green parts only

Tools

Kitchen scales	Stockpot	Small bowl
Measuring spoons	Mixing spoon	Whisk
Knife	Colander	4 serving bowls
Chopping board	Large bowl	Frying pan

Steps

1. In a stockpot, cook the noodles according to the packet directions. Drain and rinse with cold water. Set aside.

2. In a large bowl, whisk together the sauce ingredients. Add the cooled noodles to the sauce and toss to coat. Set aside.

3. In a frying pan, heat the peanut oil on a high heat. Add the ginger and garlic and cook for about 1 minute. Add the pork and cook for about 10 minutes until brown and crispy. Add salt to taste.

4. Place a serving of noodles in each bowl. Top the noodles with the pork.

Quick tip

Mincing means to cut an ingredient into tiny pieces. To make mincing ginger and garlic easier, you can use a grater with small holes instead of a knife. The grater will mince the ginger and garlic for you. But be careful of your fingers when you get near the end.

Dairy free

Nuts contains

Variation

Dan dan noodles are known for their spiciness. You can control the heat with the amount of red chilli flakes. You can also serve something cooling alongside, such as cucumbers, in case your mouth gets too hot!

Makes 4 servings
Time: About 30 minutes

Chinese sweets

At Chinese restaurants outside of China, you might crack open a fortune cookie at the end of a meal. But fortune cookies are not actually eaten in China. In fact, most meals don't end in dessert as we think of it. Sweet soups and other dishes may be part of the actual meal. Or they may be reserved for special occasions and holidays. Fruit is the "sweet" most often eaten at the end of a meal.

Steamed pears

Steaming is a traditional Chinese method of cooking. Food becomes soft and soothing as it cooks in the steam of boiling water. In a traditional Chinese kitchen, cooks use steamers made of bamboo that can be stacked on top of a wok filled with boiling water. You can make a steamer with various bits of equipment you may already have around the kitchen.

Ingredients	Tools	
2 Asian pears	Steamer (see Quick tip)	Chopping board
2 tablespoons honey	Measuring spoons	Melon baller
2 tablespoons chopped dates	Bowl	
	Knife	

Steps

1. Add water to your steamer and bring to the boil.

2. Wash the pears gently under cold water. If they can't stand upright on their own, cut a small piece off the bottom to make them flat. Then cut about ⅓ off the top of each pear. Set the tops aside.

3. With a melon baller, scoop out the seeds and cores to make small "wells" in the middle of each pear. Be careful not to break through the bottoms.

4. Mix the honey and dates together in a bowl. Spoon into the wells in the pears. Cover with the tops of the pears.

5. Place your pears in the steamer. Cover and turn the heat down to medium-low. Steam for about 30 to 40 minutes, or until the pears are soft when poked with a fork.

Quick tip

If you don't own a wok and bamboo steamer, you can use a large stockpot. Place a metal colander or steamer basket inside. Or make small holes in a foil cooking dish and place it on a cooling rack in the bottom of the pot.

Gluten free **D**airy free **V**egetarian **V**egan

Variation

Asian pears have a thick skin and are firm like apples. But if you can't find them in your local supermarket, try another pear variety, such as Bartlett, Anjou, or Bosc.

Makes 2 servings
Time: About 40 minutes

Almond biscuits

These crunchy biscuits, called *hang jan beng* in Cantonese, are sold in bakeries in China and are a popular Chinese New Year treat.

Ingredients	Tools
300 g flour	Kitchen scales
¼ teaspoon salt	Measuring spoons
½ teaspoon bicarbonate of soda	Large mixing bowl
225 g sugar	Mixing spoon
225 g vegetable shortening	Fork
1 egg, lightly beaten	Spoon
2 teaspoons almond extract	Baking tray
36 whole almonds	Cooling rack
	Spatula

Steps

1. Preheat oven to 180°C.

2. In a large mixing bowl, combine the flour, salt, bicarbonate of soda, and sugar.

3. Use a fork to combine the shortening with the dry ingredients. Use your hands to squeeze the mixture until it is crumbly.

4. Mix in the egg and almond extract. (Hands work best for this step, too.) Form the dough into a large ball.

5. Scoop out a tablespoon of dough. Roll it into a ball in your palms. Continue until you've used all the dough. Place the biscuits about 5 centimetres apart on a baking tray.

6. Gently flatten each biscuit into a circle as you press an almond into the centre.

7. Bake for 12 to 15 minutes until lightly browned on the edges. Remove from the oven and allow to cool slightly on the baking tray for about 2 minutes. Then use a spatula to move them to a cooling rack.

Ncontains **uts**   **D**airy **free**   **V**egetarian

Makes 36 biscuits (approx)
Time: About 1 hour

Glossary

Tools

chopping board	flat work surface that protects worktops from knife marks when cutting food
colander	bowl-shaped tool with holes for draining liquid from foods
frying pan	pan with a long handle and low sides for use on the hob
grater	flat metal tool with small blades used to cut foods into small strips
grill	device on a cooker that cooks food from above
kitchen scales	device used to measure the weight of food ingredients
ladle	serving spoon with a bowl-shaped scoop
measuring jug and spoons	A measuring jug is marked with lines along the side to measure liquids. Measuring spoons come in different sizes to help you measure accurate amounts.
melon baller	tool used to scoop ball shapes out of fruit
saucepan	pan with a long handle, lid, and high sides for use on the hob
spatula	utensil with a flat end used to flip food over or remove it from a pan
steamer	pan used to heat and cook foods with steam
stockpot	large, round metal pot with handles on each side and a lid for use on the hob
whisk	tool used to break down ingredients and bring air into a mixture

Terms

boil	heat a liquid until bubbles rise to the surface
condiment	food that adds additional flavour served alongside a dish
dice	cut into small pieces (smaller than chopping, but bigger than mincing)
grill	cook under a grill
knead	mix dough by folding it in half and flattening it with the heel of your hand
marinate	soak in a liquid and spices to add flavour
mince	cut into very fine pieces
savoury	not sweet
shred	cut into strips
simmer	cook over low heat so that the liquid bubbles gently, but does not boil
steam	cook by heating with steam
steep	soak herbs or spices in a liquid to give the liquid flavour
stir fry	cook in oil on a very hot temperature
to taste	amount that tastes best to you
whisk	beat quickly with a whisk to break down ingredients and bring air into a mixture
zest	peel of an orange or other citrus fruit

45

Find out more

Books

Ancient China (Exploring the Ancient World), Natalie, M. Rosinsky (Compass Point Books, 2012)

Building the Great Wall of China (Graphic Expeditions), Terry Collins (Raintree, 2012)

China (Countries Around the World), Patrick Catel (Raintree, 2012)

China (Food and Celebrations), Sylvia Goulding (Wayland, 2012)

Chinese Culture (Global Cultures), Mary Colson (Raintree, 2012)

DVDs

Chinese Food Made Easy (BBC DVD), Ching-He Huang (2entertain, 2009)

Rick Stein's Far Eastern Odyssey (BBC DVD), Rick Stein (2entertain, 2010)

Websites

Food Standards Agency
www.food.gov.uk/multimedia/pdfs/kitchen-check-yppack.pdf
Play these fun puzzles to help you stay safe in the kitchen.

The eatwell plate
food.gov.uk/scotland/scotnut/eatwellplate/#.UevoDNKsiSo
This site describes a healthy, balanced way to get all the
nutrients you need in the right proportions.

National Geographic Kids: China
kids.nationalgeographic.com/kids/places/find/china
View videos, look at maps, and read lots of information on
this interactive site.

Time for Kids: China
www.timeforkids.com/destination/china
Visit this site to learn lots about one of the world's oldest
and largest civilizations.

Further research

If this book gave you a taste for Chinese food, there are
many more Chinese cookbooks you could look at. You
could also locate Chinese restaurants in your own town or
city to try a bite of authentic Chinese dishes.

You may also be curious about China's history and culture.
Visit your local library and ask a librarian to help you learn
more. Or ask a parent to help you look up websites for
recipes, museums, or other information about China.

Index

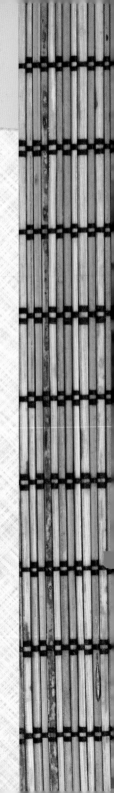